FIRE
INDEX

WINNER OF THE 2022 SUNDOG POETRY BOOK AWARD

☾

FIRE INDEX

POEMS

Bethany Breitland

GREEN WRITERS PRESS | *Brattleboro, Vermont*

Printed in the United States

10 9 8 7 6 5 4 3 2 1

Green Writers Press is a Vermont-based publisher whose mission is to
spread a message of hope and renewal through the words and images
we publish. Throughout, we will adhere to our commitment to
preserving and protecting the natural resources of the earth. To that
end, a percentage of our proceeds will be donated to environmental
activist groups. Green Writers Press gratefully acknowledges support
from individual donors, friends, and readers to help support the
environment and our publishing initiative.

Giving Voice to Writers & Artists Who Will Make the World a Better Place
Green Writers Press | Brattleboro, Vermont
www.greenwriterspress.com

Sundog Poetry Center, Inc.
www.sundogpoetry.org

ISBN: 979-8-9870707-9-6

COVER PHOTO: "Burning Crop Residue"
© Debra L. Ferguson Stock Photography

PRINTED ON RECYCLED PAPER BY BOOKMOBILE.
BASED IN MINNEAPOLIS, MINNESOTA, BOOKMOBILE BEGAN AS A DESIGN AND
TYPESETTING PRODUCTION HOUSE IN 1982 AND STARTED OFFERING PRINT SERVICES IN 1996.
BOOKMOBILE IS RUN ON 100% WIND- AND SOLAR-POWERED CLEAN ENERGY.

To live outside the law, you must be honest.

—BOB DYLAN

Freedom is a heavy load, a great and strange burden for the spirit to undertake . . . It is not a gift given, but a choice made, and the choice may be a hard one.

—URSULA K. LE GUIN

CONTENTS

I.

II.

I

Glossary of Terms

integrity, *n*. < Latin *integritās* wholeness, entireness, completeness, chastity, purity, < integer , integr- whole.

1983   A little girl walks in the side acre of the rented farmhouse. It's warm, but maybe only mid-June, so the sun doesn't press against her yet. Cows in the west pasture sidle up to the fence. She pats them hello through the weathered metal squares, feels their humid breath on her palm. Clouds make shapes—bunny, sheep, boat. Her brother's ghost is in the barn. Her big sister in school. Her mother sleeps another day away. Her father far, far away in the factory. Not one car passes on the road. She stands in a big sea of clover. Its blossoms, a rusty lavender, sweet to the suck. Her child mind. Her safe body. Sailing.

When She Introduces Barbed Wire

A seventy-two-year-old rancher
sits on the porch of my ribs,
smokes and looks out
over the vista of my organs.

It's a place of savage industry
this ranch of my body,
fusion and fission quaking.

Propping her leg on a bloodied bone
she sits on a stool up against the
ramshackle cabin of my chest.

She's been staring into my wild body for years
dog-tired but content from her day
of wrangling thoughts like bulls,
just under my skin
checking the wells for poison.

She's tanned like leather, skin roughened by the wind
hair cropped, hands callused, manlike—
or maybe it's that she's without sex,
beyond it. Freed of the need for gender.

I have spent my life on the outside
of my body being attractive to my father,
god, and other men

with serene brow, classic up-dos,
smooth legs under a flaxen skirt.
Colony Agreement: nothing is supposed to change
on the outside of my body

the waist line, the pursed lip, the hands folded
in prayer—containment, smooth slopes
pristine landscape of the distaff.

Standing at the mirror,
I push sagging skin north
tilt my head left then right, admiring
then fearing the doomed clock
of muliebrity. The rancher inside
my body kicks her boot right into my side
I double over, hear her
grumble into my gut:

Time to grow the fuck up, Beth.
It was never your face or those tits
that had any power.
It's here in the gut where
I've been laying fence. Leave
the mirror, the satisfaction of men.
Put your work boots on.

Of Birds and Bellows

The lesson the many mothers taught

                              was how to keep it up:

the house,

the dick   attached   to the man,

the ruse of tradition

                  found in things like bunting, as in   baby or banner.

To keep going, to use shallow   breaths,

anemic struts   in lock   step,

A centrifugal force of   white   women walking in circles

plumb the walls,   set the roof,

made the ideas real

                  by merely believing them.

But remember the mothers said:

stay thin

or drunk, or

         at least

         on eggshells.

Vie for diamonds,   for yoga

retreats in the Cayman Islands.

Something

        to type home about on your phones.

Do not look   outside   your own construction.

Lately, my sabotage takes place in the garden, as in   pulling weeds
up   by the roots.
When I refill the birdfeeders
I am   really
                weaving nests for the children.
I teach them silly   songs about wings
                        and hunting.
                        They collect
yarn and ribbons.
        We say it is for   craft. It is a gift
not to be paid
attention.

In night dreams   we slip through
the screening,   barefoot with my breasts
hanging
low
I set up temples made   of yew branches. The children
hop   from limb to   limb   on the nearby   tree.
All around the paper-thin house

                        the stacked cards
                        of history
                        tremble.

I light
        the temple fires.   I light
        and light.
From high on the fir
                tree the bird children
                and I, their mother,   call.
The breeze answers

like bellows.

QUIET// ALL OF THE TIME

sometimes I wonder
        whether I call these memories
up from my loneliness or
do they,   like shadows of the dead,

        wait behind the curtains
        in the pool of oil in the frying pan
        inside the sheet billowing

                my hands press and smooth the
            bed of my brain
and there: there they are:

ghost braille // of over-turned milk pails,
        old baby suitcases   opened, satin
        stippled with swallow's shit,
        the old Edsel we used to play in
with the dead mice all over the floorboards,
the mildewed hay in the barn loft   clogging my ears
        packing my mouth—

        so quiet //   all of the time—like God

        or our mother.

This Is Also True: Dream #34

The tar-and-chip road a cat's tongue under bare feet.
Yellow in hair and in fields,
rich honey of sun, swaying grass.

Then: my brother in a field to the south,
a boy and happy.
He stays long enough for us to understand

that he can go now
that I can too
that maybe suffering doesn't matter as much as it once did.

The road licks my feet, nudging me.
I keep moving—knowing he is safer now—
no longer haunting the fence line of my heart.

If you drive east toward Packerton Rd
you might still see him running as the deer.

Thunder Cell

In the early 80s when people stood in lines for dolls,
my stepsister and I got girls. My big sister
got a boy named Kyle. Looped hair and overalls.
I remember my daddy lynching him
with a shoestring noose wedged in her door jam
because she was getting both older and a mind of her own—
He'd laugh and laugh and we'd laughed too.
Because the man who'd whip us
for nearly nothing, he was laughing. And because
I didn't want my doll up there in that door jam.
Sometimes we'd find Kyle in the microwave.
Sometimes my daddy'd swing him by the toes
and fling him against the wall.

For a hot minute, we felt equal to our father, and better than
something smaller and weaker than us. I'll be honest.
So honest I heave for the shame of it—
it was a genuine relief.

Glossary of Terms

hypocrite, n. French hypocrise< and intimation of a person's speech< Greek γλωσσο- hypo—under *comb. form* + -λαλία sift, < λαλεῖν to speak. *hypo* meaning under, and *krinein*, to sift or decide. From root *Krei*—to sieve, therefore discriminate, distinguish.

1984   Her father used to preach about loyalty. In long talks, he explained the meaning of 'hypocrite' in Greek, because he was in seminary, and everything went back to the Greek and the Hebrew. Being two-faced was the worst thing you could be, the opposite of faithfulness, or goodness. So she nodded and cried and said how sorry she was for sinning, scared to reach down and feel the hot welt rising up from the leather of his belt. A little girl caught looking in his wallet. She wasn't stealing, there was never any money. No, she was just curious about the things forbidden to her. What later she'd come to name as the shape of power. When she couldn't take one more stripe, he'd swoop her up. Cradle her, kiss her crown, rock her as she sobbed. Being repentant felt safer than being beaten. Almost like love. That's when she took herself a secret, a secret that kept her alive in his house: lying is more like choosing, with a bent sieve in one hand, and the other on the door.

Glossary of Terms

altar, *n.* < classical Latin *altāre*. Raised structure used as focus of worship in a Christian church (*c*1100 or structure used in Israelite and Jewish worship; raised structure on which to sacrifice offerings to a god, noun of an unattested adjective< the base of *adolere* to burn, cremate.

A slot in the backdoor of Heaven we push all our prayer through, hoping for something back; a place for the tit-for-tat.

1978   A young man and his wife love God. And they are devout in their beliefs. They believe it wrong to rely on anything other than God. The Big Guy has all the answers, and the more you please the Big Guy, the more blessings slide through the slot of the door. And they pray for everything. And because they have such a strong faith that the Big Guy does everything for them, and requires a non-compete, they pray instead of taking their baby to the doctor when he gets sick. And they pray. And they pray. The Big Guy does nothing. So they pray harder and watch the baby as the spinal meningitis wraps around the cord of his back. And they pray on their knees at the Big Guy's back door. They show God how much they love him and trust him and only him, to save their baby. They are waiting for their miracle. They are waiting for the exchange. They are eye level with the slot in the door, the altar as a mint green crib, the slab on which they sacrifice something precious. For weeks they let the baby scream, no longer able to move his head. He goes deaf. He goes blind. He eats his own shit. Fever burning up his brain. When the child dies, my mother peeks through the slot of God's back door. Nothing. The angels have all cleared out.

There Is Nothing That You Can Do to Save Anyone

One week after their home caught on fire
she sits at a red light,
her kid in back with a hospital bracelet on.
Who would have thought a walk in the woods
to breathe fresh air, to exhale smoke and grief
would wind up with a tick bite
on the boy's ankle,
spread into dark blooms
all over his body in a matter of days.
In the little cabin they've rented—
convinced carbon monoxide has killed her children
closed up in the next room—
she stands sniffing.
She remembers a story passed down
through the knitting of her bones—
how before she was born,
her parents drove up highway 24
to see the patriarch.
That night the baby boy woke crying, then the girl.
Their father, angry at the shame of unruly children,
fearful of waking his own father,
punched the girl quiet. Their mother was
vomiting and falling. Then the grandfather woke up,
took one look around, opened all the windows,
muttering about the furnace
and found ice for the three-year-old's eye.
Those first two kids in Michigan,

they didn't make it. One is still alive,
sure, but her heart was beaten
clear through. The child born after her brother's death,
this mother looking in on her kids in a stuffy cabin,
left to make a family that she would protect,
a family she could save—
Even they burn.

She needs it quiet

Mom's taken to the animals now and the snow because they mistake her for the silent trunk of the tree and expect no warmth. A basket holds shrunken heads of fruit. Candlesticks wrap themselves in dust, pages in the photo albums cover each other's mouths. Stories hold their breath in this place. The deer and the mouse and the rabbit—they know to squint lest the black of their eyes shine too loud a wildness. They lick the bark of her toes. They drop dumb pellets all along the hall. Heads hang low as the winter drifts in, banking against the stairs. If the animal startles: pain's heat, felt first in the palm and then burning at the eye sends our history screaming.

> Dead brother of mine:
> do you see how it is now,
> after you are gone?

So There I Was in My mind, Driving Like Hell All the Way to 1978

Then brother, long dead
but living in my head,

> you said:
> *Step on the gas.*
> *We must all go back again.*

Then:
Stop!
And: *See ! See !*

Your infant crib
an altar in chipped mint green,
and there you were, writhing.
Fever cooking your brain.
Our big sister, palms pressed to her ears,
muting your screams.
Our mother and our father
kneeling, pushing play on
Brother Freeman's voice so sure
as he spoke of healing *in the name of Jesus.*
With one hand on my shoulder

> you said: *Pick me up. Sister. Please.*
> And: *Hold me as I die.*
> *They won't even notice—*
> *their eyes were always closed.*

When She Tells Me the Dangers of Conflating Myths

The rancher who lives inside my body sits by my collarbone, so I can hear her.

Remember that time the man who forced your legs open, showed up a year later outside the bar you'd go to to get drunk? He lit your cigarette, then you up and drove him to your apartment. What were you doing changing into a long white cotton nightgown—what were you trying to get, resting with your rapist like it was an Act of God?

But you've been trying to conjure rainbows all of your life, haven't ya? Trying to wield the waters back in their place after the levee broke, turn the clock back, even before you were born. Who are you really wanting to save?

You know going backwards doesn't reverse shit. Acting out some myth your daddy told about you being a sign of forgiveness—a sign of his new beginning after what he'd done.

Baby, I'm gonna tell you real slow so you can hear me, that's horseshit—trying to turn a girl into a mercy.

That bow of colors didn't appear in the sky to cover over wickedness in the world. It came to say never again.

I know how hard you try. But you will never cover any man's sin, hold it in like an ark. And God's mercy? It doesn't happen by going back in time—forcing it pure by turning a blind eye. It happens by the great flood of sorrow washing us out, drowning us up to the top.

Bloated, eyes peeled to what *is*.

OF RELIGION

the making too long
stitches hastily sewn only to be pulled
what is left?

now, but then always too: a pierced collection
                    of desperate apertures
a lace of mis-aim
        of pricking genuflections

godde,
we have made and unmade you
        (in) the image of our violence
threading the needle with our broken bodies—

Glossary of Terms

glossolalia, *n.* < Greek γλωσσο- glosso- *comb. form* + -λαλία speaking,
< λαλεῖν to speak.

The phenomenon of speaking in an unknown language, especially in religious worship.

1991   It was winter when the traveling preacher came to stay at
our apartment above the church. She was with us for three
weeks, every evening leading prayer in the Fellowship Room
downstairs, interpreting the prayers of those who had come,
and laying hands on the bodies desperate for God's touch. I
was supposed to be asleep, but the singing and the praying in
tongues kept me awake, awaiting the presence of God. I could
really feel something, coming like the winds before spring.
Something wild. I snuck down the hall to the stairs, tucked my
knees into my flannel nightgown. I can still feel the cold skin
folding over the bones while I tucked the hem under my toes.
I lifted my head, prayed what only my heart could sound out
syllables of a lonely child: *oteesh-sha-na-ka-la-   o-sheekitee-
too-kal-a-   backa-shem-kal-lata-   jeku-ma-la* And God.
God obliged, and gave great company.

THE CLOCK

He pins my sister to the wall, gripping her jaw.
He keeps asking her what time is it?
Her girl body straight like a pole under the clock
scared because she doesn't know how to read radial.
He keeps at her, *what time is it?*
What   Time   Is   It?
whattimeisit? whattimeisit? whattimeisit?
And my mom's voice, begging.
Please, don't do this. He doesn't pause.
My sister is sobbing, his hands like clamps,
like his jaws set on teeth, grinding down
something no one can see.
My sister clouds over, no movement in her face,
snot runs out her nose, tears soak her navy-blue sweater.
My dad getting more and more
energy in his voice every time he asks,
what
time
is
it?
like there is some sort of electricity
he's harnessing, sucking the life out of her.
I am standing right next to him, silent.
Willing the answer to her brain, desperate to end
this. My dad like a light bulb—hair shining,
beams out of his eyes, his hands almost glowing.
He turns to me. He asks, (you can hear

the sick smile in his voice) *what time is it, Bethy?*
My dad radiating with a goddamn corona
around his head, and I, because I served
at the pleasure of his shining, answer. Exactly
right, because he's taught me all week how to count
by 5's, while my sister's at school and mom at work.
He lets my sister's shoulders slump,
the light and fury somehow gone,
drained as he lets go, done with her.
Picks me up. Talks about how smart I am, how
even a four-year-old can read a clock.
My sister looks ashen, burnt out,
standing there staring at the sweeping second hand.
He leans down over her. On his hip, I swing down.
My cheek brushes her hair, one last shock stings my face. And
he says, *You are an idiot,*
real low and measured in her ear.

Thursday Afternoon

You know, we didn't stand a chance. Cards stacked up against each other like floating fish, dead in the bowl. When the boy gets home from school today, he'll go into his room and find colorful scales decomposing in the putrid fluid I know I should have changed weeks ago. And he'll cup the water, watch the carcass of his first pet ride the current down into his palm. He'll take his index finger, the one he'll use later in fury—the kind only grief can charge—and point it at me. But for now he uses it gently to caress his fish's belly. Listen to how he's calling it by name—like a body might come back from the dead just because it hears pain and regret but now we're calling it love. Listen to how he's calling his loss love. Begging to be proven wrong. If I could bring that fish back, have it flip its tail on his skin, if I could blow the word remorse into my own mouth to revive the dead inside of me, surely I would.

LET ME BE CLEAR: THE DREAD

did not come on at marriage for any of us—
for we were always our father's daughters.

I have seen this in the women in my line,
        stuck only to stories authored by men—
tales like flypaper hanging

                in

                        my grandfather's garage.
Their names,   their empires made from hauling lumber or
leading people to Jesus. The women,
they just waited

                eating grapefruits, or easier—nothing at all.
Always pregnant. Always hungry.

II

Glossary of Terms

suburban neurosis, *n.* < Brit. *suburbyn.* A set of psychological and physical symptoms, said to occur particularly amongst suburban housewives, associated with feelings of boredom, anxiety, loneliness, and lack of personal fulfillment.

2015   Tonight I sit with a friend and drink gin while she talks about her mother and her grandmother dying of cancer. We talk about jewelry and other women in the neighborhood—just another way to talk about cancer. The third round of drinks is yet another way. I text my running partner—*I won't make it in the morning.* I text the babysitter—*go ahead and put the kids to bed.* Tomorrow afternoon, I'll pick them up from school, read books, play games. My husband will come home and I'll serve the latest vegetarian experiment. We'll have a dance party in the den. Saturday I will drink hot tea—visit my friend at her garage sale. Neither one of us will say a word about tonight. We'll stay silent as we squint in the morning light. Our children will run around the card tables set out in the yard with bric-a-brac piled everywhere. The cicadas will buzz. The sun, scream.

When She Tells Me About Shams

Last week in the middle of doing morning chores,
me at my kitchen sink, her weeding my liver, she says:
To worship suffering is just a con.
Life isn't sweeter, the honey doesn't drip quicker
because the bear feels the sting on her snout.
She wags a finger at me. I drop my head, listen.
I know what she's saying is true:
Always making it about yourself—that's the hook,
ain't it? Your kid's birthday and you spent more
time telling about your trials laboring them.
It doesn't matter, how long or how bad the pains were.
It doesn't matter you were alone or that he nearly ripped you in two—
what matters is the glory of them being alive,
standing witness to mystery becoming flesh.
Stop taking yourself the pain, lady-girl.
Don't you know women who wear the badge of suffering
don't have room for anything else?

Glossary of Terms

smoke, v. Old English *smocian*. To produce or give forth smoke.

2013   When my father told me no one would ever love me as much as he did, I believed him. Even after I was full grown. Because he was god and could make the reins snap against my back, jerk the bit in my mouth. Use the call words I was trained with and everything but him would disappear. All my life he fed me apples from his mouth to my eye—teaching a filly to go blind is a kind of steering. My job: chattel for the master. But then, standing in the stable I tipped a lantern. Bursting bright in the hay. Big eyes reeling round and round the barn of his beliefs. After I burnt it to the ground, I walked out into the wilderness. When I meet another animal, hide also worn from the harness, she asks me if I know my coat is still smoking.

Instead, We Set the Fields on Fire

I look forward to a long talk with you finally after we're dead, our ghost legs flopped over a blackened sill. The storm window with its rickety metal ridge no longer cutting into the backs of our thighs, like it did when we were young, perching over the porch roof to see the moon of the young corn. It'll be cool summer nights forever—Indiana, crickets singing—freight trains fat with silage howling across the flat land. Our ghosts will smoke cigarettes together. And we shall sit, our spirits willing a heft into our backsides as we inhale. And because we're ghosts, the tar smell won't seep into our hands or hair as it did when we were sisters—sure signs we weren't the good girls we'd been raised to be.

We'll be dead then, so we won't have to lie. We won't have to avoid talking about the nuances of love and violence we were born into. How need and want and touch and hate bundled our bones for kindling.

Horses Broke Loose

Like the light in a darkened wood,
plash on leaf, siloed warmth in shadow
air between canopy and clay,
her memory brightened and blinked
particulates of the past, slideshow
motes of when she believed she loved him.

> Coffee'd and sun-screened today's morning
> promised hot. The garden lush with weeds
> duty-pulls her out across the paddock.
> Then: whir of chainsaws. The neighbor,
> clearing her horse yard so mud can dry
> (happy hooves, happy horses).

Gravel grinds underfoot, coffee mug sloshing
so loud the tree breaks, crashing   light everywhere.

She had mistaken her desire for love
as the thing itself.   The horses broke loose.

Prayer for Something Else

for Tara

My friend reminds me
I have to sweep the floor
before I can put lace on the table,
and I know she's talking about us.
You and me, Lord.
And I wish I could skip all this
and lay out the feast,
crimp the pie, feel you close to me again,
like I did when I hated myself.
I could feed you from the fork
of all my wrong-doing, and it would be called
love or devotion. But, God, lately I've been thinking
love might not look so mutually exclusive,
like me wanting to die, and me wanting you to live.
Maybe love doesn't look like you
having to die so I can live either.
Like, maybe I've been loving you wrong.
What I want to ask, Lord,
what I want to say so much
that my heart is squeezing my throat
and stinging my eyes is this:

Will you help me sweep my religion away?
Can you become a woman, and I a stag?
Can you become a tree, and I a song?
Or maybe a pregnant cloud,
and I the rain?
Turning into each other
turning out of each other over and over?

LIVER SPOTS

the little islands floating   in the surface of my face
dark like   cloud

each little mass a coagulate of   memory

like the liver heavy of all the years
holding starts to   weaken   releasing

glob by glob through the water of   my body
past the murky sea creatures of   jealousy
        or her sister   hunger
past the monster inside me called   love

an ink cloud billowing in a frozen glass

        on the forehead   a whole scattering
of them freckle and chatter
        laugh at me for the years
I took myself seriously
and then for when I didn't

the blood   pools   and   pitches
for every time I danced
or took off my clothes
        or let sweetness into   my mouth

Bruised iris blooms for all of my   misunderstandings

these little descansos
along the buried veins   my face a map called treaty

there are more prayers on my face than pores

belief is always mottled
                    with grief, doubt, and   hubris

I wonder if you lick my skin if it tastes   like regret
I wonder if you sucked these little   tips
of cold volcanoes, could you pull up   hope

Glossary of Terms

writeress, *n.* Old English *wrítere* , < Old High German *rizari*, etc., painter (German *reisser* tracer). A female writer or author; an authoress, a revealer of secrets, double agent, mandated reporter.

1923   A woman looking almost white in Swartz Creek, MI. As a little girl, she learned to suck in half of her bottom lip, always wore a big hat to ward off the sun. That little girl, trained in white ways, hated her mother for never coming close to her, saying she had to keep her distance. By the time she married, she was abandoned to her migraines from an overbite—terror of her secret. A hatred and fear in the shade of her privilege.

2007   My grandfather dying of cancer is hopped up on a morphine patch, drinking boxed apple wine. It's late at night. I'm sitting there, 3 x 5s scattered everywhere as I'm trying to write this down. He says:
My mother was a mulatto. Passed for white and never let slip a word about it. Then one day my father found a manuscript she'd written in secret called The Seed Bed, *all about passing. Well, my father was so mad, he burned it right in front of her. Don't ever fool a man, Beth. But if you do, don't write about it.*

AFTER THERAPY
(or Do Not Confuse Reluctant Acceptance of the Child With a Rescued Marriage)

We had driven to the beach to sit in the car. Just to get out of the house during the quarantine. I told my husband I found striped palazzo pants on sale for Ash. Ash goes by 'they' now. But my husband said something about jeans and t-shirts. I knew we weren't supposed to talk about it. We need to keep our dates neutral. Try not to fight. I sat there with my sandwich in my lap, a heavy stone in each lung, and the lake view through the windshield. A few birds were diving together. The breeze big enough to fight back wings. I said, I don't think Ash really wants jeans. They don't like the way pants feel in between the legs.

We looked at the water, how the wind cut it into sharp angles, steel gray, serrated. I wondered how often birds drowned in the search for what they want. If the other birds save them. A woman wearing a mask walked along the road. I balled my hands in my pockets, ducked my face into my collar to feel the warmth of my breath. After a while he said, almost to the birds, *I remember now reading about the crotch thing in a book about raising transgender kids.*

GHOST PRAYER

for now.
let me just say this: when you   dear girl
discover the door at the back of your mind,
the one without a bell
the one without a lock
the one draped with rosaries   made of words
smoking from the friction
of gendered dreams
go ahead   walk through it.

all the women in our line
while folding sheets
or slicing meat
while reeling in childbirth
or the shuttling of sex,
          have all been weaving   an amulet
that you might be set to fire
and not burn:

yarn of an unraveled baby's blanket,
dirt from a grave speckled with mica,
the ten moons of your mother's hand,
eyelash of a doe, a window   called hunger,
bead of sweat,   whimper of   prayer—
          the cold clay of   courage.

it's ok to go away for a while
          and to (please)   come back

Spring Theology

A glass marble rolling down the painted porch floor:
    an act of forgiveness.
Rhythm lurching every wooden seam:
    a remembrance, an inertia.

God, you are my slanted velocity.
You are the black dirt of my childhood:
    a graveyard of marbles.

On cool nights,
when you and I exhale, God,
out comes a joined body of shadow.
Together, we are so desired by the air,
that it might ravish the very prayers
we have for one another.

My prayer: moonflower and spade.
My spade: the sound of worship,
    shushing against soil and glass
    scraping grace for even myself.

You are the particles in the darkness of my body
    in the darkness.
Your prayer: the wood, green leaf and bloom.

Weeding the Garden

My loneliness is a train howling one and a quarter miles away from the window. It usually pulls in at night, although, loneliness can arrive mid-morning or afternoon. Today, it is 2 o'clock. The station is behind the sternum. There is a gap where my other organs have not barged in. I consider loneliness an organ, one that wheezes along in a cave of darkness; the organ is the empty space inside the cave. Sometimes the space, that is to say, my loneliness, swells against the walls of the cave. This is the feeling of grief. Grief is not located in the heart, but in this dark and swelling loneliness. I sigh, and my daughter says, "What?" And I say, "What?" To this she answers, "Mama, you sighed."

I do not tell her that I fear my marriage to her father will end, or that my life has been a series of misunderstandings. I do not tell her that the empty drumming space of loneliness only quiets itself when my hands are in the dirt which makes me wonder if my only relief will be death. (Isn't death Infinite Loneliness?) I do not let myself wonder out loud if the answer to my loneliness is loneliness.

If it is, then my marriage is saved for I have never felt lonelier than with my husband. I do not tell her I've felt lonely all my life: in the middle of revival church meetings, or with rich people in rich schools, or even while birthing her. Loneliness, like the lung, or the appendix, was there from before the time I was born, developing in my mother's womb. When I think about this, I do not quote the passage in the Bible where God says He knew me in my womb. I have always found that verse to be quite cruel. Unless God is, in fact, Infinite Loneliness. In which case, things make much more sense.

I turn from the window, and look at her, a budding lonely girl herself. I say, "Come out to the garden with me. Let's weed the plants."

Instructions for October

Collect it all in a 50-gallon drum.
Other people's secrets you've told, all the times
you believed in your own innocence.
Or when you let the fruit rot on the counter.
When you lied to the man you loved
or you nursed the baby while drunk.
Put them in

with the dress your father made you,
then his fist on your fontanelle.
The day you wrote your new name.
Birthday parties in the yard,
dance-offs in the kitchen.

And don't forget
the beauty of your 17-year-old
body. Or the victory of the first time
you jump-started a car.
When all your babies were born alive.
Started telling the truth.
The homemade jam. All that.

Find a kitchen match—old fashioned.
Remember when you actually used them.
Embrace your age, and that you came
from nothing. Strike. Light your cigarette
and then toss the torch on your tender frailty.
Watch it flicker and smoke. Then catch.
Warm your hands at the heat.
And thank god.

As Wind

My chest
was tearing   most days because

my love for you was   too big. As a child, I tried
to cut my skin loose, right

              at the wrist—trying
to make

a little more   room to fit   my devotion. Because
        you loved me.

And nothing   frightened me more
    than you   and the absence of you.

And that was the way it was,
me keeping small,

with shallow breath to make room
        to host your many ideas of me

inside my body. Often,
I lied to us both. I said I liked

diminution, but
I grew into myself and   out   of my self

several times, when you weren't looking.
It has taken years

to drag you all the way out of my skin. It has taken
years   to tell the truth. To love

myself more than anybody else. The truth
is I am growing large and rightly foreign.

I used to think
loving meant knowing
so well one could guess every desire,
every wish delivered   before utterance;
so one could   surprise and   conclude

at the same moment. Look, a foal in a field.
Look, a bowl of pecans in dusty light.
Now love is as bulbous as a papered wasp nest,

as striking as wind.
                    I cannot imagine myself.   I can not.

In Medias Res

Right now a scrap of birch is curling into the night. Right now the kid chews chocolate that's over a year old found in the bottom of a moving box, turning a page so dry and thick you can hear the index finger drag. The comic book borrowed from the library, the throw blanket piled on the pajama'd lap like a tired animal. The story, full of illustrated boys with quick wits, speed lines behind their shoes, neatly drawn in their action boxes, speech bubbles, drawn-on smiles. The kid nibbles the chocolate right down to sparkly painted nails. Wonders about friendship, about those perfectly drawn boys in their boxes. How after being held down on the snowy playground it's hard to be in close spaces, one boy pinning shoulders, pinching nose, covering mouth, how another boy straddled the middle, taking to the chest like a punching bag. The kid now thinks about those boxes—how boys are friends inside. But there's no box big enough for all the dresses and skirts borrowed from sister, or the new ones Mom bought in the right size afterward, no box big enough for the long hair, the climbed trees, Dad's silence, and the snow forts to fit boys who feel like friends to a boy who doesn't feel exactly like a boy.

In the night that is happening exactly now, over and over, the birches have started moving, black lines in a black sky, delineation lost except to the papery husk gently peeling away. The kid, looks up at the silent mother because it's annoying to be stared at, golden hair flipping a little like bark off a birch, book closing with what you know will leave smudges. The kid with round eyes says, *Mama it feels like the world's closing in on me and I can't breathe.* The mother pockets the candy wrapper as she scooches closer, so careful to not scare the kid. And now, there is a period of silence between them as they listen to the wind outside.

Go ahead and listen.

They hold hands, breathe. Their diaphragms moving gently, their bodies imperceptibly swaying. Their collected atoms the same as the ones in a cluster of trees.

She says, *it's ok baby,* even though they both know it doesn't feel that way. She says, *it's time you brushed your teeth and hit the hay. Go on.*

When She Tells Me to Grow Up

The rancher inside me
does all the heavy lifting
while I'm off feminine sidesaddle skirting
what I don't want to look at. She's the one
who knocks down my lung-door at two in the morning
waking me up in a cold sweat
to remind me that this American dream
I finally got is just trumped-up scam marketing
my survival mind made.

She only startles me awake
when it is quiet enough for me to imagine
rats in the air ducts. A phobia so strong
I wonder how much I want it to be true.
How much I want to be able to relieve my mind
and say to myself, *Ah yep, I knew it. Fucking rats
this whole time.* So I lay there waiting
for her to tear through some fascia,
some construction, I've made from habit
over and over, making the resigned
genuflections of my toy womanhood.
She usually tells me there are fucking rats
in the barn of my heart again because I haven't
shoveled the stalls for over a week now.
Do the work, she says.

But tonight I'm already awake before she
tugs at my paranoia like a long-roped bell.

Something's wrong, and it's not in the crawlspace.
Between my legs, a fever is coming on,
and soon enough, I'm up pissing hot red shame.
Bladder screaming, *infection*. Screaming, *pay attention*.

What now, I ask, because I can feel her
leaning on my sternum. She's getting tired or maybe it's old, I can't tell which.

She says, *Beth,*
you're god damn killing me with all this guilt,
it's flooding the fields and I can't get seed to stick.
It's okay you changed your mind.

I walk her inside my heart—
lay a quilt over her resting body,
sit on the edge of her narrow bed.

What do I do?

She motions for me to light her cigarette
as she spits into a blue bandana.
Then pats my knee.
Remember the first time you heard my voice?
You were in front of a mirror
doing just what your daddy taught you to do
counting up all the ways you should hate yourself,
sleuthing around for something wrong.
What did I say?

I lean over and take a drag of her cigarette
smiling at the memory. You said, *Grow*
the fuck up, Beth. Get some discipline.

Glossary of Terms

discipline, *n.* <Middle English *discipline.* Senses relating to punishment, to training, instruction, or method to mold the mind and character and instill a controlled and effective manner.

Then: Spare the rod and spoil the child.

Then: Train the child in which she shall go, and she will not depart from it.

Now: Broad blade of grass, late summer. Light crawls with the calculated risk of a wolf spider, no web to snare the oncoming frost. This is my practice: to succumb to all I have left done and undone, get low with the weight of self-pity, bent so south, I take a hard look at my bunioned feet. I decide to love them, my feet. I decide to love the grass they're standing in, and the cold morning dew, the fire that I'll pop them up toward in a month, and the lake they sloshed around last Monday. I practice deciding all day long. Shame and remorse cower in their low gravel cough of addiction. I decide to love them too, those sad beggars. They die completely taken by surprise every night.

Animalia Dea

Behold, I crouch at the lich and call
in the clearing of the woods named America

I lick the eyelid
of your secret name—

To summon a spell to wake your body
inside the body abandoned

To lift the hem of your skin
to the other side of you

Oh Woman, turn the spoon of your own gut
Light a lamp in the first body—

Inhabit the deep pools and hot thrum
the body before the ichor set clear

Make again milk from milkteeth
Tongue babies like language—

spill them from your body lips
to fill the home of your ancient temple

With the body daughters of your mouth
I want to chant in the cathedral of your bones

Great Mother, come back home to the body—
Blink open the stars, set your feet down

tip the trees like scales.

Forgiveness sometimes

is a fray of light from velvet
        feathers—
red-winged blackbird,
        bejeweled birch tree.
Sometimes it is how I walk right past.

Testimony

                                    Every so often,
during an eclipse, say,
don't you wish you had stayed out
in the desert,
the desert with cold night clouding
black across your face, the desert where
you left her for good—the Mother Godde
stirring fires in the earth, the mother
who set the griffon flying north?

                                    She
was quite the cook, your mama,
feeding you wild wool, spun dream
& danger. Under her feet sprang pools
of water. Her shawl of oblivion. *To forget,*
she said, as lightening crackled from her teeth,
to forget is the only power
you possess. The other gods and I do not have it.
She bundles you up good for the long walk
away. *Remembering,* she warned,
will break you.

                                    It's been years
now, many thousands. You've come to America
and you do American things. Sit in a recliner,
look out the curtained window.

The sprinklers on sod, the alarm systems
easeful. Your lungs sluggish, your heart
wrapped in fat. Tribes starve somewhere. Paved
roads clog with protest. Your children
do not visit you; they're even better at forgetting.
                                        But then.
The blond white Jesus wind-up doll,
the one on your shelf for good luck,
your talisman so you don't have to think.
Well, light like thunder starts shooting
out of the valve of that Jesus and you hear
the voice of the Mother and you feel fingers
renting the mantle of your mind in two
as she says, *Here we go, baby, for*
your own good. Meet your brother . . .
and your wind-up Jesus, your little
slave of each-prayer-a-twist, comes toward you,
turnin' over tables left and right,
                                        and you see:
The Queer Violator of Religion. Dancer in the Desert.
Daughter of the Mother. Beloved of the Father.
Your own heart rattles cracking desert hot light.
And you, you remember.
Jesus, how you remember.

HOME, OR RETURN, OR SAFE

There are deserts where my ribs should be–
blank   areas of a map,   a vast empty echo.
As a child I learned the parts that would keep
me alive.
          The eyes to see my father
the ears the cunt the breast
                    my mind to keep everything   separate
in their place, dis associated.
          When my physical therapist asks me if
I feel pain   I don't know how   to answer
                    I do not know how   to locate
my knee,   I do not know how   much load   is too much
or how this even
          has a goddamn thing
                    to do with my lower back.

☽

Isolation requires a certain   silence   between parts.
A purity code of solitary confinement.

                              (Beware the infectious nature
                              of communication)

☽

I wonder about my friend in middle school,
   if we had just told each other about   our bodies,
     (who had eaten their fill,
     who were still hunting.)
Maybe then our strong slick blood could have obeyed
the deep drum of breath. The blood
   could have sailed vascular rivers,
over the sloped tendon to cayoneer the sockets
     all the way to our frightened feet.
The message clear as oxygen: supplies on the ready.
   The flesh so turgid we could have run   forever.

❨

The plan was to fill the head with ideas—
   an insular barrier,
   a sort of barring of the door
     (right at the mouth.)
A disconnection so severe,   the only messages
that get over the gates now   are hyper-aroused flares,
missives from the peaks and valleys of sex and injury.

❨

It is a great rebellion for a woman to inhabit her own body
   a return to her native language
   that cannot be captured—
a language   before language of towered symbols
   like: wedding rings, wrinkles, and framed degrees.

☾

I have discovered sinew under
my right breast, left calve, arm pit,
middle back
       rich with relationship,   each fiber
strongly woven like a braided ladder
      of hair
           cell wall to cell wall.
                          Muscle, bone, plasma.
All the nerves blink in the sky of my body
       a reverberation   and an absorption.
A call and response throbs
       mystery at my temple.
Something deeper than song—
       called home,   return,   or   safe.

Divorce

Forget the woman I was
I must lay her down among the worms
:

       turn the earth over in order to dream a new fence line.
A new field.

When the summer comes

I'll walk into the woods north of the house.
The neighbor will meet me at our boundary
line—point out the good wood brought
down by yesterday's storm.

The chainsaw with that new blade makes
light work of an oak and two birch.
The kids'll help stack, grumble this is worse
than weeding—they won't know to give a damn
for the oil bills come November.
Their beautiful arms tanned.
Their faces flushed.

Later we'll unwrap sandwiches in front of the lake.
Somebody will complain they didn't want mustard,
while the other searches for cell service.
We'll joke some. We'll see how fast we can swim to
the buoy. Then on the drive home, windows

down so the wind can dry our hair,
I will choose this life over and over.

Glossary of Terms

Fable, n. < French fable < Latin *fabula* discourse, narrative, story, dramatic composition, the plot of a play, a fable, < *fārīto* speak: **see fate** *n.* **FATE:** The primary sense of the Latin word is a sentence or doom. A fiction invented to trick; a fabrication, falsehood, secret truth.

2020   When the revolution finally arrived, windows busted through, the lawns gashed with fire—inherited memory, ancestral lies, the folktales we told ourselves of innocence and godliness, all fell like ash and laced the abandoned bones, the bleached seeds found inside the belly of that earth. A scrap of fur nailed up on the pine—broken glass scattered on the ground—strips of linen tied to laundry lines. The leaders who survived, they handed their signet rings to the gardeners.

      Men began to bare babies like the seahorse. Women grew tails like wolves. When a true memory now comes to visit a village, it comes as the old infirm. It is nursed and cared for in a hammock made from the villagers' hair. Everyone bows to the loom where the body is held. It is from this cradle where the body of memory sounds out a song. No one forgets. When the body is burned, our own heads blister.

Fire Index

Altar (see; *sacrifice*)
Alter (see; *memory*)
America (see; *gravel*; see; *plow*)

Barbed Wire (see; *boundary*; see; *open field*)
Body, of earth (see; *integration*)
Body, of woman (see; *open field*)
Boundary (see; *marriage*)
Brother (see; *ghost*)
Burn/ing (see; *home*)
Bury (see; *plow*)

Children (see; *sacrifice*; see; *home*)
Christianity, of white America (see; *burn/ing*)
Cog in wheel (see; *woman*)

Daughter (see; *vegetable seed*)
Desert (see; *home*)
Discipline (see; *misunderstanding*, see; *open field*)
Divorce (see; *altar*, see; *open field*)
Fable (see; *hard truth*, see *memory*)
Family (see; *open field)*
Father (see; *misunderstanding*; see; *sorrow*)
Fire (see; *fire*, see; *fire*, see; *fire*)
Forgiveness (see; *marriage*)

Ghost (see; *white-tailed deer)*
Godde (see; *open field*)
Gold (see; *godde)*
Guilt (see; *sin*; see; *silence)*
Gravel (see; *children)*
Home (see; *quiet)*
Hard Truth (see; *gravel)*

Integration (see; *open field*)
Lung (see; *forgiveness)*
Livestock (see; *live stock;* see; *cog in wheel)*
Live Stock (see; *misunderstanding)*
Loneliness (see; *bury)*

Marriage (see; *altar,* see; *open field*)
Memory (see; *sorrow,* see; *boundary)*
Misunderstand/ing (see; *family)*
Mother (see; *snow)*

Open Field (see; *Godde;* see; *burning)*
Plow (see; *restitution)*
Quiet (see; *snow)*
Responsibility (see; *woman)*
Restitution (see; *lung;* see; *guilt;* see; *fire)*

Sacrifice (see; *misunderstanding)*
Silence (see; *sin)*
Sin (see; *sacrifice;* see; *burn)*

Sister (see; *snow*)

Snow (see; *sorrow*)

Soil (see; *home*)

Soldier Bird (see; *forgiveness*; see; *body of earth*)

Sorrow (see; *open field*)

Tower (see; *snow*)

Turn (see; *livestock*)

Vegetable Seed (see; *forgiveness*)

Water (see; *hard truth*)

White Tailed Deer (see; *lung*)

Woman (see; *snow*)

Winter (see; *open field*; see; *body of woman*; see; *open field*)

ACKNOWLEDGEMENTS

Thanks to the editors of these journals for believing in the poems and giving them safe passage.

"Let me be clear; the dread"— *The Boiler Journal*

"When She Tells me about Shams"—*The Helix Magazine*

"Instead we set the fields on fire"—(in a different version)—*Up North Lit*

"Prayer for Something Else"—*Forklift*, OHIO

"Spring Theology"—*Letters Journal*

"In Medias Res"—*Chattahoochee Review*

Thank you to Sundog Poetry Center and Shanta Lee for believing in this book; to Neil Shephard and Rebecca Starks. Thank you Dede Cummings at Green Writer's Press for making it real, and keeping it real. I will forever be grateful for the teachers and friends who supported me while I made the poems. Thank you for your mentorship, encouragement, tough talks, and care: Laure-Anne Bosselaar Brown, Nickole Brown, Tina Chang, Mark Cox, Betsy Sholl, and Natasha Sajé. The MAAB forever: Melissa Lowrie, Alexis Groulx and Andrew Hahn. Collin Berry, Julia Alter, and Meaghan Castle. My heart to Tara Campbell. Sheila Rigg, everything good to you. And finally, to my family chosen, given, and taken: like the tides, I take you in, I give you back. I choose this every day. I love you, Emma Jean. I love you, Ash.

About the Author

BETHANY BREITLAND was born in northern Indiana. Her people are cult members, truckers, doctors, child-mothers, and business tycoons. She has lived, studied, and taught on the West Coast, the South, and New England. Breitland earned her undergrad degree from Pepperdine University, and her MFA from Vermont College. As an educator and activist, she has worked for over 20 years concerning women's rights and the LGBTQ community. Recipient of various poetry prizes, this is her first full length book of poems. She lives with her children and her partner Michael outside of Burlington, Vermont.